Wild mouse

IRENE BRADY

CHARLES SCRIBNER'S SONS,
New York

for my sister Diane

April 6.   *I've just seen a*
wild mouse—smooth, sleek,
darting across the sinktop.
I'm going to try to sketch him.

April 14.   *I'm trying to win his confidence with*
cornflakes and apple chunks. If I'm very quiet
he stays in sight long enough for me to sketch a little.

He fits the description
for *Peromyscus leucopus*,
the white-footed mouse,
in my field guide.

April 20.　*Two weeks of constant coaxing,*
but it was worth it. He sat and ate sunflower
seeds in my hand tonight, but when I moved
slightly he was gone　　*! What a delightful*
feeling, those tickly toes on my palm!

When he's nervous
he hugs the floor.

April 30.   *He's getting so tubby I can't
believe it! Maybe I should stop feeding him,
but he's so beautiful to watch (even though
he is fat)....He's building a nest someplace.
He's made a total wreck of the toilet paper roll.*

Could "he" be pregnant?

May 5. He is a she! I pulled out the drawer of the coffee mill because I heard scratching inside and I'm watching a small miracle. She chewed a hole in the back of the mill, built a snug nest, and is crouched in its hollow having babies. One tiny red thing lies beside her and another seems to be coming. The mother is ignoring me. She's busy.

The baby is tiny—maybe only
an inch and a half long
including the tail.

It just crawled clumsily
under its mother—maybe
to nurse? It's 1:08 P.M.

1:16 P.M. *Eight minutes later...*
the second baby has been born now,
with the mother mouse watching very
closely and licking it thoroughly.

Now she's bitten the umbilical cord through
and is eating the afterbirth. It looks like
a disk with a rolled edge.

side view

I guess the rolled edge is what
rolled back off the baby—like
peeling a sock off a foot....
Just got a look at the first baby
again. Its skin is transparent.
I can see the white milk in its
stomach and dark pupils
through its eyelids!

milk inside
stomach

1:28 P.M. *Twelve minutes later...the mother mouse is asleep now. Both babies seem to be nursing and the mother is having some labor contractions. The contractions are so strong they make her whole body ripple. It's about forty seconds between waves. They keep waking her up.*

1:30 P.M.   *The third baby just popped out
tail-first, really fast, and the mother is
licking him. Who'd ever guess these ugly,
salmon-pink things could grow up to be
beautiful wild mice?*

Her tongue is just a blur.

1:38 P.M.   *It only took the third baby eight minutes to get to its mother's milk. They're all nursing now— legs beating and kneading in rhythm with their sucking. Their ears are just lumps. The tips seem to be fastened down over the openings. They have tiny whiskers and eyebrows. Their toes are stuck together except at the very tips.*

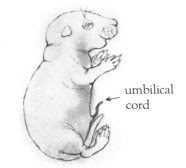

umbilical
cord

Tail is neatly
curled up under belly
most of the time.

right
hind foot

(I had to quit sketching. The mother mouse woke up and got very distressed when she saw me. More tomorrow, I hope!)

May 7. Two days old. Their skins are
so loose they flop. Mother is gone, so
it won't bother her if I sketch. One baby
is scratching its head with a hind foot
but can't keep upright. No coordination.

Scratching is hard work!

They're so lively. They look like
they're made of red rubber. I can
see the blood vessels in their
feet when I hold them to the light.

The babies are still hairless
except for eyebrows and whiskers.

May 9.   Four days old. Their ears have come unstuck! They're starting to groom themselves. They try to sit up but keep falling over. The front toes are separated but not the back toes. The babies are moving around in the nest a lot.

This one was washing its face.

Color is starting to show. Brown hairs are sprouting on their upper parts and white hairs on the undersides.

May 10.   Five days old. They're getting fat but still
don't fill up those loose skins. My sketching visits
disturb the mother so I do it when she's gone.
Sometimes when she leaves the nest she drags a baby
out attached to her teats—they really hang on tight!
She carries them in when she notices.

3 inches

May 12.   One week old. I can see their two-tone coloring
clearly now. Their skin is nearly covered by fur.
They're chubby. They've filled those loose skins and
the coffee mill, too.
They're about three inches
from nose to tail tip. I've just noticed something about
their ears—although the tips came
unstuck when they were four days old,
the ears are still sealed inside.
I wonder how well (or even if) the
baby mice can hear....

These two
fell asleep
in my hand.

May 16.   *She moved them. It took me a few days
to track them down. They're eleven days old now
and she's having trouble keeping them in the hole
in the old chair cushion she's using as a nest.
They're active and wiggly, beautiful wild mouselings
with fat tails and sleek coats.
Still blind. Ears are opened now!
They're about four inches long.*

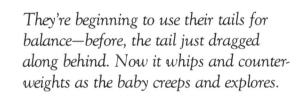

They're beginning to use their tails for balance—before, the tail just dragged along behind. Now it whips and counter-weights as the baby creeps and explores.

May 19.   Two weeks old. Four bright eyes gazed at me in astonishment today when I lifted up the loose cotton from the top of the nest. The third mouseling is still in its blind baby-world, but these two are on the brink of growing up. Now that they can see, they're afraid of me. They jump like crickets ⟶ at a sudden movement or sharp noise.

May 21. Sixteen days old. I saw
a movement from the corner of my eye
as I sat reading...

and there was the mother mouse leading a skittery line
of babies toward the cupboard where the oatmeal stays.
I always leave an open box of it on the shelf for her.
Now she's teaching the little ones to forage.

*They still nurse, but altogether
they weigh more than she does.
They look like miniature adults
with tiny ears and too-short tails.*

When they all nurse at once they
lift her right off the ground.

May 31.   *The little family has left its nest.*
Mama seems to be getting "tubby" again.
Under the table two bright black eyes twinkle
up at me, crunching sounds come from the
oatmeal cupboard, and there is a whisper
of tiny feet from the attic—these
things tell me my wild mouse
family has grown up.

Library of Congress Cataloging in Publication Data

Brady, Irene.   Wild mouse.
SUMMARY: Text and drawings document the pregnancy of a wild
mouse and the birth of the babies.
1. Peromyscus leucopus—Juvenile literature.
2. Reproduction—Juvenile literature. [1. Mice. 2. Reproduction]
I. Title.
QL737.R638B67   599'.3233   76-14912   ISBN 0-684-14664-9